Connie's Gifts- Interactive Books and Collectibles
Got Challenges?
Book 2

How to: Deal when you Think you Cannot Deal.

Some helpful tips to assist you in the right Direction.

(Includes practice skills, exercises and worksheets for learning, teaching and growth).

Offering Support for those Individuals, Children, Parents, Teachers, Counselors and Helping Professionals, dealing with day-to-day struggles, as well as, those, working with individuals diagnosed with Autism, Mental Health Disorders and Intellectual and Developmental Disabilities.

Before, During and After the Pandemic!

Book 2: Focuses on Healthy Coping Skills, Increasing Self-Confidence and Self Love!

Let's Move Forward!

Constance Jackson, M.Ed., LPC

Connie's Gifts- Interactive Books and Collectibles. Got Challenges? Book 2
HOW TO: DEAL WHEN YOU THINK YOU CANNOT DEAL. SOME HELPFUL TIPS TO ASSIST YOU IN THE RIGHT DIRECTION. (INCLUDES PRACTICE SKILLS, EXERCISES AND WORKSHEETS FOR LEARNING, TEACHING AND GROWTH). Offering Support for those Individuals, Children, Parents, Teachers, Counselors and Helping Professionals, dealing with day-to-day struggles, as well as, those, working with individuals diagnosed with Autism, Mental Health Disorders and Intellectual and Developmental Disabilities. <u>Before, During and After the Pandemic!</u>

iUniverse books may be ordered through booksellers or by contacting:

iUniverse
1663 Liberty Drive
Bloomington, IN 47403
www.iuniverse.com
844-349-9409

Because of the dynamic nature of the Internet, any web addresses or links contained in this book may have changed since publication and may no longer be valid. The views expressed in this work are solely those of the author and do not necessarily reflect the views of the publisher, and the publisher hereby disclaims any responsibility for them.

Any people depicted in stock imagery provided by Getty Images are models, and such images are being used for illustrative purposes only.
Certain stock imagery © Getty Images.

ISBN: 978-1-6632-2498-9 (sc)
ISBN: 978-1-6632-2499-6 (e)

Library of Congress Control Number: 2021913321

Print information available on the last page.

iUniverse rev. date: 03/25/2022

Contents

Dedication:

This book is dedicated to my God, my husband and my family. To my husband, Clyde Jackson, the love of my life, who changed my life in a way I could have never imagined. You have supported all of my endeavors. You are my angel and my hero. To my children: daughter, Freddricka Jackson and son, Burnell Neal Jr. I am blessed to have you. You helped me to become a better person and mother. I adore and cherish you both, always. You gave purpose to my life. I am so grateful and proud of the adults you have become. To my son-in-law, Jaqua J. and daughter-in-law, Brooklyn N. I am grateful for you, love you much. To my siblings (and their spouses) Thank you to Denise P., Cornealious P. Jr, Norma B., Nethel P. and Nina F. You are the ones I have always looked up to my entire life. Thank you for your support over the years and I love you forever! To my nephews: Paul B., Marcus P., Zachary P., Christopher L., and Troy M., you are and always will be special to me. Love you forever.

All honor to my paternal aunts and uncle: Lola Petitt-Fowler, Wilma Petitt-Hill; Roy S. Petitt.

In loving memory of Ivory Petitt, Anna Petitt-Jones, Harrison Petitt, Nethel Petitt and Vivian Petitt-Miller.

In loving Memory of my maternal aunt, Jannie B. Rogers. Our parents, Cornealious E. Petitt Sr. and Annie Johnson-Petitt, who I will forever love and be grateful to you both, for doing your best in raising six children. We are blessed to have the best of both of you! Rest in Peace. Last, but not least, thank you to all of my cousins and close friends, especially Pamela R., Isaac K. Sr. and Angel K. I am so proud of you and your accomplishments. I love you, always!

Constance Jackson, LPC, M.Ed., Author

My Note Page:

Special thanks:

I would like to say thank you for your interest in this book collection. Thank you to Dominique H., Daliah S. and Brooklyn N. for their expertise, and assistance with completing this book collection. Thank you to by father-in-law, Mr. Elliott Blocker, for his support, encouragement and words of wisdom over the years. You are awesome! Thanks to all of my past and present professors, supervisors, colleagues and co-workers for their support.

Disclaimer:

This illustration is strictly for support of others and not intended to take the place of a licensed therapist, providing therapy or counseling sessions. As with therapy, clinicians and author cannot guarantee any specific results. Treatment success depends on you, the individual in which services are being provided. Seek medical attention from a helping professional, if at risk of harm to self and/ or others, by contacting 911 or going to your nearest emergency room.

Description of Book:

As a helping professional, I dedicate my life to helping children and their family to the best of my ability, to facilitate empowerment and hope for a brighter future. ----*During difficult times, therapy is not always the first choice and, in some cases, not easily accessible. There are several reasons people hesitate about therapy, such as the negative stigma of seeking help for mental health and mental illness, cost, lack of compatibility with therapist, location, insurance issues and now due to social distancing, during the Covid-19 and Coronavirus Pandemic of 2020.

This interactive book was written with the aim of supporting those individuals who are supporting others. Its main focus is to help individuals, parents and helping professionals in need of support, when assisting others (e.g., children, teenagers and adults) dealing with mental health conditions and challengingbehaviors. Additionally, during this time of the Covid-19 Pandemic, this book offers support to those whoare unable to go into an office, for face-to-face visits and those who are unfamiliar with working with said population. This interactive book is intended to help and support those who are having difficulties managing their thoughts, behavior and emotions, while coping with life changes, stressful situations, mental health conditions and IDD challenges.

This book or any therapy services cannot guarantee any specific results, outcomes or promises, but may facilitate you and/ or your family member(s), to tap into your own power and strengths, to reach personal goals.

Everything you need is within you! This illustration contains demonstrates and describes some activities and exercises that can be used in the schools, home and community settings to begin the process of self-awareness, healing and moving forward.

Therapy is about self-awareness and developing coping skills to navigate through life's challenges. Being a helping professional, for thirty-five plus years, I realized I do not have the physical capacity to work endless hours, to help all of the children and families I would love to help. By writing this book, I can share some of the information and techniques that I have learned, used and acquired over the years. Some have proven helpful in assisting hundreds of children, families and adults. For me, this book is like my version of the story of "Saving the Starfish." If I can help one, maybe I can make a difference in one person's life and even for the next generation. My version of the story is not helping people, one by one, but putting these skills into a written form, to share with all of those in need, simultaneously, maybe even around the world. I hope this information reaches you. Remember, there is always hope!

Note: in the book, functional coping skills will be underlined, to indirectly provide guidance and prompts to functional alternatives to manage challenging and difficult situations and behaviors. It also includes positive affirmations to increased self-confidence, and self-worth. The narratives and instructions may be used for guidance as you complete each exercise. Be empowered tomindfully implement some of these healthy alternatives and coping skills into your daily living.

About the Author:
Constance Jackson is a Licensed Professional Counselor, who completed a Master's Degree in Education, Specializing in Community Counseling and successfully passed the National Counseling Exam (NCE). She is qualified to counsel under the guidelines of Texas States Board of Examiners of Professional Counselors.

Her formal education was received at University of Houston- Main and University of Houston- Victoria. Work experience includes the following facilities: Schools, Day Programs, Community Centers, and Hospitals

(Inpatient and Out-patient settings). She has helped hundreds of individual and families through conducting individual, group, family and couple's therapy.

Work Experience:
As of 2021, Counselor Jackson has worked 36 years in MH/ IDD (Mental Health/ Intellectual and Development Disabilities) Services. She has worked in private practice, various health care settings as a Behavior Intervention Specialist, Voc. Habilitation Manager, and Counselor/ Therapist/ LPHA/ Clinical Treatment Director of a Residential Treatment Center, all with the purpose of supporting and assisting individuals and their families. Lastly, Counselor Jackson has experience working with persons of varied ethnic, racial, sexual orientation, and religious backgrounds. One of her goals is to aid those she can help, when others have turned them away. Her moto is, "If I do not help, who will. So, I will try." So many people are in pain, some due to past and present events. Some have been harmed through generational trauma, but there is hope through intervention, psychoeducation, access to resources and helping children and their parents/ family, to develop steps to achieve their personal and family goals.

Theory of Counseling

Counselor Jackson adheres to a combination of three frameworks of theories: Cognitive Behavior Therapy (CBT), Rational Emotive Behavior Therapy (REBT), and Solution Focus. For CBT, developed by Dr. Aaron Beck. Cognitive Behavior Therapy focuses on the interconnection of your thoughts, behavior and feelings and how they affect the other. The goal is to reframe those thoughts for a more positive perspective. 2). The Rational emotive behavior therapy (REBT) approach to counseling, This theory focuses on the here and now, This theory focuses on the here and now, not past or future events, and refuting irrational thought and beliefs. (REBT) also focuses on educational and learning processes. Learning or teaching individuals new thoughts and behaviors patterns, resulting in possible resolution to the problem that brought you here today. 3). and Solution- Focus realm, developed by (Shazer & Berg) techniques may be used to reinforce successes and assist the client in gaining self-confidence and self-awareness with a clear focus of the client being the expert over their lives, and working within their own story; working to assist individuals to find alternatives to a more fulfilling life. The goal of therapy and this illustration is to assist individuals to reach self-awareness through an evidence-based approach. In this illustration the author will provide you with additional information, concrete examples and interactive exercises, that will hopefully assist you with challenging behaviors in the home, school and communicating setting, if consistently applied. This illustration does not make guarantees, but may offer some guidance, support and hope by developing potential alternatives to reach personal goals.

Narration: As we enter into Book two, let us explore the topic of coping skills and how they help us.

You are worthy!

CBT: Coping skills:

Coping skills can be spending time with your favorite people, places or things, that help you to manage and reduce the effects of challenging situations or emotions.

After learning some valuable coping skills, from the previous book, here's an exercise.

"Challenging your negative thoughts" is a coping skill that is very effective, for most people."

If you have a negative thought, what should you do?

Accept it	OR	Challenge it
"go with it."		"fight it."

*Write your answer here: _____

Exercise: Ok, let's see if you learned this lesson. How can you challenge these negative thoughts?

1. I am bored? (ex. I have a lot I can do and a lot to be thankful for.)
   Now, write down your example of challenging the thought, "I am bored." "_____!"
   (Make a sentence here)

2. Nobody likes me. (ex. My family loves me.)
   Now your example of challenging the thought, "Nobody cares about me." "_____!"
   (Make a sentence here)

3. How does your new thoughts make you feel? _____ (emotion)
   (name your emotion)

Note: The sooner you use your identified coping skill, the better you will feel and the sooner we will feel relieved of your difficult situation and uncomfortable emotions.

You have resilience!_____

Coping skills: Is it Facts or Fiction?

Note: When you challenge a negative thought, challenge it with the facts.

Do you have evidence or proof that the thought is true?

Scenario: "She said I was ugly. So, I must be ugly. "

*Let's challenge this thought...

Example: "I look like my mom and father and they are both beautiful people, inside and out. Therefore, I am beautiful."

Fact: 1+1=2
Fact: "I am beautiful."

- Note: Beauty is relative, based on certain societal norms. Who defines your beauty? You or Others? Select your choice. "___ define my beauty."
  Answer here.

- Coping Skills: <u>Do not internalize the opinions of others</u>, because they are only that, their opinions, not facts.
- Test your thoughts with facts, not feelings. You will feel better.

Note: If the negative thought you are having is true, "replace it". It is not doing you any good. It does not work. It is dysfunctional.

Narration: This worksheet may be used to help identify healthy and enjoyable coping skills that you may utilize to stabilize your mood and/ or increase your quality of life.

You are a Queen! _____ You are a King!

Is it Facts or Fiction?

(+) Positive thoughts add to your joy.
(-) Negative thoughts subtract or take away from your joy.

Minimize the negative events in your life, by <u>engaging in positive activities</u>, <u>talking to positive people</u>, <u>getting rest</u>, <u>eating healthy</u>, <u>staying hydrated</u> and <u>getting proper sleep</u>.

<u>Positive self-talk</u> and <u>positive affirmations</u> are also effective coping skills.

Example/ Practice: Read these positive statements out loud and then check your mood. Practice daily.

"I deserve love." "I love myself." "I love you." "I am ok." "I am awesome."
Remember, You Deserve to Be Happy.

Below, identify what activity makes you happy?

Circle the ones you can use as a coping skill. Write or draw your own list of things that make you happy below. These can be considered your coping skills and can be used as a visual reminder when needed.

_____

My Coping Skills:

1. _____

2. _____

3. _____

4. _____

5. _____

6. _____

7. _____

8. _____

9. _____

10. _____

Note: Make sure your thoughts, behavior and feelings are congruent (the same/ match). If you want to be happy, exhibit behavior to make yourself happy (e.g., making good grades, doing homework, following rules, setting/ respecting boundaries, spending time with family and engaging in your favorite hobby).

Key Point: It is also helpful to rely on a higher power and/ or to believe in a power outside of yourself. Prayer and meditation are essential coping skills.

Narration: Sometimes, we take ourselves too seriously. Now, let us tap into your humor, be social and/or find your happy place, to regulate your mood. Use this demonstration to practice.

Great Job! You are Awesome!_____

Regulate your Mood! Be Happy!

Note: Do something each day to make you happy.

Draw or list activities that make you happy. You can even draw your "Happy Place."

Exercise: Practice: Learn a new joke that you can tell to a friend or family member.

*Write your joke here...

- Homework exercise: Practice telling your joke to someone, like a friend.
- Note: Laughter makes the heart grow fonder and improves your mood.

I am Unstoppable!

CBT Cognitive Triangle
CBT- Developed by Aaron Beck.

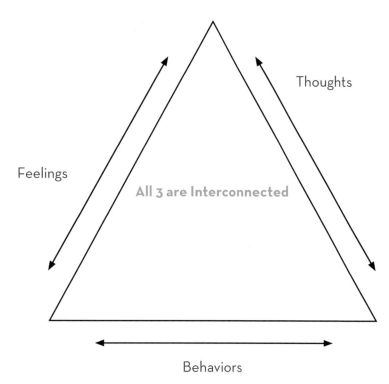

Feelings

Thoughts

All 3 are Interconnected

Behaviors

"Self-Awareness!"

"Self-Awareness "is very important, essential for growth and maturity. Self-awareness can also be very difficult. Commonly, the human mind and ego is designed to protect itself. People get distracted by other people's problems and issues, because we fear dealing with our own, hurts, pains, history of traumas, shortcomings, mistakes, fears and goals. Let us face our own fears and challenges.

Recommendation: Talk to a professional that will help you work through and process those unresolved issues, feelings and thoughts. We sometimes cover up, bury and take unresolved issues or emotions out on those closest to us and/ or those who love us the most. You deserve peace, self-love and forgiveness of self and others. Be free to live and enjoy your life.

<u>Self-Evaluate</u>.

Tell me about you.

Know yourself.

Your thoughts.

Your Behavior.

Your Feelings.

Your motives for your actions.

Your fears.

Your dreams.

Dr. Aaron Becks developed the Cognitive Triangle, which can help you explore your thoughts, behavior, and feelings. Each one affects the other.

- Exercise 1: On the next Note Page, self-evaluate, by describing yourself using the statements above.
- Exercise 2: Today, I recognized how my thoughts affected my behaviors and mood.

"I felt _____, because I _____."
ex. happy ex. saw a friend.

My Note Page:

_____

_____

_____

_____

_____

_____

_____

_____

_____

_____

_____

_____

_____

_____

_____

_____

_____

_____

_____

Narration: Use this exercise to continue exploring and challenging thinking errors with the facts.

You are Wonderful! _____

"Exploring a common Thinking Error- Jumping to Conclusions"

*Notes: Every belief or thought you have is not true. They are called Automatic Thoughts.

Example: 1). She/He will not like me.

Challenge the thoughts.

Is it true? _____
How do you know? _____
Is there evidence? _____

Example: 2). I think she/he is talking about me.

Challenge the thoughts.
Is it true? _____
How do you know? _____
Is there evidence? _____

Coping skills:

Communicate, ask the person, have patience, wait to see outcome and minimize the situation.

Examples of Positive Self-talk: "It's ok. I'm ok, I'm good. They have their opinion and I do not have to accept it." Tell yourself, "Everyone will not like me and It is ok. I will not like everyone and it is ok. We can still respect each other."

Note: Even if a thought is true, is the thought functional? <u>Yes</u> or <u>No</u>

Does it work? <u>Yes</u> or <u>No</u>

Does it help you? <u>Yes</u> or <u>No</u>

Does it make you feel good/ happy? <u>Yes</u> or <u>No</u>

Answers: Communicate, ask, challenge the thoughts, check the facts, by talking to the person directly.

Note: If you answer "no" to 1 of the questions, use the space below to replace the negative thought with a positive thought.

Use the space below to replace the negative thought with a positive thought.

Complete the exercise here.

I am Extraordinary! _____

Use Positive Affirmations to Regulate your Mood!

Positive affirmations can help manage feelings of depression and anxiety and regulate mood.

Examples of positive affirmations:
1. **I am so awesome!**
2. **I am smart!**
3. **I can do it!**
4. **I got this!**
5. **I'm valuable!**

Write your own positive affirmations in the blank space below.

6. _____.
7. _____.
8. _____.
9. _____.
10. _____.

How do you feel when using your positive affirmations?

<u>Bad   Same   Better</u>   (circle one)

If you answered the same or bad, go do an activity that makes you happy or spend time with someone you love. It is easy to focus on the problem. Let focus on a Solution!

_____

Note: Daily Practice. Use the Likert Scale (Developed by Rensis Likert) to monitor your mood and self-evaluate. Use a scale of 1-10 ("1" is saddest you can be and "10" is the happiest you can be). Take control of your mood. If you are a '2', do something about it. You can do it!

1	2	3	4	5	6	7	8	9	10

Narration: This demonstration focuses on increasing your self-confidence and spending time on yourself. You are worth it. Let's give it a try.

You are Powerful!_____

 Increase Self-Confidence! *Self-Confidence to Deal with Bullies-

Time is Money Approach

Let's look within ourselves. <u>Spend time on yourself</u>. You are great! Show others you have <u>self-love</u> and that you care enough about yourself to spend time and energy on someone that is valued, loved and important, You!!

Forms of self-love: Time is Money for Self-Confidence!

*self-care   *shower   *clean clothes   *wash-face   *comb hair   *brush teeth   *sleep hygiene

*do not skip meals, because of others   *eat healthy   *do homework   *clean your room   *exercise

*listen to your parents and teacher   *make good grade   *study
to pass your test   *take care of your property

*communicate when you need help from others   * stand up for yourself
and your rights and rights of others (with support if needed).

Do not give bullies, your time, attention or your energy.

It's not easy dealing with someone that bullies others. Mostly, bullies target those who want your attention, attention from others, have low self-confidence, high self-confidence and/ or have some other underlying issues. Often, they lack the ability to respect the healthy boundaries of others. Therefore, you may have to <u>set some boundaries, but the choice is yours to make. Healthy boundaries keep us safe and others safe.</u>If others are bullying you, it is not your fault, but it is your responsibility to care for yourself.

Tell someone what is happening to you. It will be ok, but if you do not tell someone, chances are, it will only get worse. It is better to be safe, than sorry! It is risky to bully and even more risky not to tell someone what is happening to you. Do not give your time and energy to those people who do not deserve it.

I hope you know that their behavior is not about you, but how you handle this situation IS… Be mindful of what is going on with you and around you.

Coping skills: Communicate, ask for an adult's help and set healthy boundaries. Your voice is your power, make eye contact, use calm and firm tone when communicating, do not over-react and give lots of attention to the bully.

Scared Mouse

Soaring Eagle

When people see you, what or who do they see?
Circle one, or draw your own image in space below.

<u>Narration: Here is an illustration that depicts someone being overtaken by the influence of a bully. Explore... Use this demonstration to facilitate change of how you see yourself. Remember, do not focus on what others may think.</u>

You are Powerful! _____

Increase Self-Confidence!

What do you see when you look in the mirror? A person that has high self-confidence and high self-esteem or self-low confidence and low self-esteem? Circle which statement describes you.

If you recognize your low-self-confidence that is progress, because of your increased self-awareness. Now, you can do something about it. Only you can fix it, if you recognized it and/or acknowledge it!

Coping skills: Challenge the negative automatic thoughts and your negative core beliefs, about yourself.

If you realized you need to make some changes, Give yourself a hand! I am Proud of you!!

Increase your self-confidence to deal with bullies- Time is Money Approach

Insecurity is like a magnet for bullies.

You are valuable!

Do not forget it!

Narration: This illustration focuses on knowing your own self-worth. If you do not know it, who will? Let's explore.

You are Valuable! You are Worthy! _____

Self-Worth!

Webster defines the following:

Self-confidence- feeling of trust in one's abilities, qualities, and judgements.

Self-esteem- feeling of satisfaction of one's self and his or her abilities.

Self-worth- sense of one's own value as a human being.

How do you present yourself to others to show your own value? _____.

Circle the behavior that you demonstrate.

Do you <u>hold your head up high</u>, <u>look them in the eyes</u>, <u>talk with firm voice</u>, <u>show respect for yourself and others</u>, <u>make healthy choices for yourself</u>, <u>set boundaries</u>, <u>self-care</u>, <u>stand up for self</u> and, **(add one)** _____.

Self-confidence & Self-esteem

1. <u>First, spend more time on yourself</u> (remember time is money!) Most people spend time on things they care about. <u>Self-care and self-preservation are essential for a happy and balanced life.</u>
- Compare and self-evaluate how you spend your time. Do you spend more time on video games,homework, job, self-care, exercise, television, focusing on others and their opinions or strengthening your own mind, body, personal goals, gaining knowledge or reading? **Circle those that apply. Do you have balance?** Yes or No?
- Do you focus and worry about others (family or friends) or do you focus on yourself and your self-care? Focusing on yourself is not selfish. <u>It is brave to work on your own issues.</u>
- <u>Be mindful</u> and <u>Be humble.</u> If you do not care for yourself, you cannot help others.

Coping skills: (e.g., hygiene, prayer, meditation, organizing, school, making good grades and being your best you).

Equals

Note: You are worthy of your own time and time from others.

For children and teens, you have the right to ask for help and the time of others, especially from parents, without having feeling guilty and without thoughts of infringing on their rights Increase your chances of success, by asking your family and friends for help. They may appreciate you sharing.

Do not Silence your Greatness for anyone, including yourself.

Self-Worth!

The more time you spend on you, the more others know you value yourself. Not just focusing on material things, but focusing on your self-care and self-love, by spending time on yourself and putting yourself first.

Write how you show self-love and value to your life _____.

Write how you show love and value to the life of others _____.

How to show signs of self-love and self-care:
Here are some Examples:

Be responsible	Clean clothes		
Drink H2O	Do what you want, over what others want.		
Exercise	Brush teeth	get rest	
Doing homework	Eat healthy	Sleep Hygiene	
Study	spend time with a friend	Making Good Grades	Take a class
Set boundaries	go for a walk	Showering	

Note: If you love yourself, it is easy to love others. Put Self-Love in to Action each day...

Narration: These next illustrations demonstrate how one's thoughts, behavior and feelings should be congruent versus incongruent to reach personal goals.

Taking Risk = Growth = Success! _____

Self-Love!

Example: If you want to be promoted or elevate yourself to the next level, be it school (e.g., elementary, middle/ high school, college) or a job, you would be very happy and proud. Yes, you deserve that feeling! Be mindful to try. Do not give up on yourself.

Your thoughts, behavior and feelings must match. The three components must be congruent (e.g., the same or equal) in order for your desired outcome and desire feelings to be achieved with ease or less difficulty. Consistency is an important element for success.

If these components do not match, it will be more difficult to reach your goals. Let's take a look...

Here is an example of incongruent thoughts, behavior and feelings. Note some of the consequences in the "feelings" column.

Thought	Behavior	Feeling
• I want to pass my grade. I want to graduate.	Sleeps late, do not complete homework, do not study, poor test grades. Absent or do not log in to on-line school/ class.	I want to be happy, but poor grades make be sad. I get in trouble with my parents. My parents do not trust me. My phone and games are taken away. **"I am not very happy."** Some may experience depression, anxiety, stress and disappointment.

Note: Remember this is an example. Use this chart to generalize this exercise for other life situations. See below.

• I want a promotion on my job.	• Late for work, miss deadlines, break rules, insubordinate	• Disappointed with work record, demotion, lack of respect from co-workers and supervision, no raise or promotion.

* Note: This behavior is not self-love, but self-defeating. Would you want others to make you feel this way? Why do it to yourself?

*How likely are the chances you will reach your goal of getting promoted and being happy, with this incongruent behavior? __**Poor** _ **Fair**_ **Good**_ **(Circle one).**

_____

Exercise: Are you being <u>congruent</u> or <u>incongruent</u> with thoughts, behavior and feelings? Rate your likelihood of success, On a scale of 1- 10

1   2   3   4   5   6   7   8   9   10

You are Bold! _____

Self-Love!

Increasing self-motivation can come from reframing our thought processes and making thoughts, behavior and feelings congruent. Now, Let's take a look...

Example of Congruent, thoughts, behavior and feelings. Note some of the consequences in the "feelings" column.

Thought	Behavior	Feeling
• I want to pass my grade. I want to graduate.	I wake on time, I complete my homework, I increased study time, make high test grades. Be present in class, in-person and on-line. I log in to class on-line each day.	I am happy and proud of myself. My parents or happy and not worried about my future and education. I do not get in trouble, but get rewards and free time to myself, because I am responsible and my parents trust me. I have my phone and games. I am very happy. I feel loved, by myself and others."
• I want a promotion on my job.	• Early for work, meet deadlines, follow rules, Team player.	• Proud with work record, respect of self and from co-workers and supervision, raise or promotion granted. Happy, Accomplished.

Let's re-evaluate.

Answer the following questions. Is this behavior self-love? Circle: Yes or No

Is this behavior self-defeating? Circle: Yes or No

Would you want others to make you feel this way? Answer: Yes or No? What is the reason for behaving this way toward yourself? Explore: _____.

*How likely are the chances you will reach your goal of getting promoted and being happy, compared to the previous incongruent behavior? __**Poor _ Fair_ Good_ (Circle one).**

_____

Exercise: Are you being <u>congruent</u> or <u>incongruent</u> with thoughts, behavior and feelings? Rate your likelihood of success, On a scale of 1- 10

| 1 | 2 | 3 | 4 | 5 | 6 | 7 | 8 | 9 | 10 |

Note: <u>Asking for help is a strength</u>! Do not be afraid of asking for what you need to be successful. Utilize your internal and external resources to be successful!

__Narration: This exercise can be used to practice asking for help and to introduce roleplaying activities to practice learned skills.__

Be Truthful to Yourself and then You can be Truthful with Others! _____

Self-Love!

Exercise: How would you ask for help if you are having trouble with making good grades? **Let's Roleplay.**

Practice "Hi, I need help with_____, would you please help me with _____."

Note: It is very important to do roleplay, homework and practice the learned coping skills with the individual. These things should be completed for their knowledge and to increase their comfort level when using the new skills.

My Note Page:

Narration: This information can be used to explore and identify resources to meet needs, as a coping skill, and to minimize stressors.

I am Blessed! _____

Exploring Internal and External Resources!

There are two types of resources internal and external resources. A resource is a power, which we use to meet our needs. We have to recognize and tab into the power source within us and outside of us, (e.g., in other people, places and things).

Note: Generalize using internal and external resources for various situations. See the charts below.

1. "I want to make good grades." Explore and develop coping skills by identifying and implementing your resources, as functional coping skills:

Parent/ Teacher: Assist individual with developing their own diagram.

Internal (Resources)	External (Resources)
Positive Self-talk, "I can do it."	Teacher
Take action	Parents/ siblings
Increase study time	Computer
Do assignments	Books
Do research, google	Library
Communicate with others	Counselors
Ask for help.....	Therapist
Self-care- Sleep, eat healthy	Friend/ Study partner
Add more...	

2. "I want to get a job." Explore and develop coping skills by identifying and implementing your resources, as functional coping skills:

Assist individual with developing their own diagram.

Internal (Resources)	External (Resources)
Do job search	Get referrals from teachers and others
Complete applications	Use computer/ websites for jobs
Communicate for help	
Add more...	

Note: Remember, <u>using your resources is a strength</u>, not a weakness. We all need others. Therefore, sometimes, not asking for help can be identified as a weakness.

__Narration: Continue to explore and identify resources to meet needs, as a coping skill, to minimize stressors.__

I am Fortunate! _____

Exploring Internal and External Resources!

3. "I want to have a healthy friendship or relationship." Explore and develop coping skills by identifying and implementing your resources, as functional coping skills:

Assist individual with developing their own diagram.

Internal (Resources)	External (Resources)
Self-love	Communicate with family and friends
Set and respect healthy boundaries	School
Self-care	Work
Try new things	Social events

4. "I am having depression and anxiety." Explore and develop coping skills by identifying and implementing your resources, as functional coping skills:

Assist individual with developing their own diagram.

Internal (Resources)	External (Resources)
Self-care	See Doctor
Challenge negative automatic thoughts	Therapist
Take medication	Nurse
Keep appointments	Family and Friends

Note: Remember, you do not have to recreate the wheel. Generalize learned coping skills for various events and situations.

Narration: This illustration explores coping with uncomfortable feelings to increase self-confidence and recognize how those feelings affect you and others.

We have to Keep Dreaming! _____

Building Self-Confidence as a Coping Skill!

Note:

- If you can <u>visualize it</u>, you can do it!
- If you know how to <u>utilize your resources, challenge your thoughts and reframe your thoughts</u>, these coping skills may increase your self-confidence, which in turn will help you with building friendships.
- Have positive body language.

Example:

1. Look people in the eye.

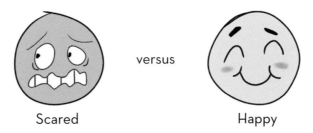

Scared versus Happy

If you are uncomfortable, it usually makes the other person feel uncomfortable for you.

- Be Yourself! It will be ok! You are ok!

Question/ Exercise:

- **Which face belongs to you, when talking to others? Scared or Happy?**
- **Explore and challenge the thought, if you answered scared.**

Coping skills:

1. <u>Minimize talking to others</u>. You can do it! It is only a big deal, if you make it a big deal. <u>Control your thoughts</u>. <u>Do not Maximize and Blow things up, (in your mind)</u>, but <u>minimize the situation and the thought</u>. We are all the same. Different, but equal.

2. <u>Work through your uncomfortable feelings</u> and push through. Afterward, you will feel better about yourself. **Key point: Each skill learned builds on the next. You are headed in the right direction.**

My Note Page:

_____

_____

_____

_____

_____

_____

_____

_____

_____

_____

_____

_____

_____

_____

Journal your thoughts.

Forward!

We are all Equal! _____

Building Self-Confidence as a Coping Skill!

3. Challenge negative core beliefs/ negative thoughts about yourself.

Here is an illustration of a person named 'Freddie.' He is standing alone, watching a group of children play. He is saying to himself,

"They won't like me."

Children talking and having fun with each other.

Coping skills: Freddie <u>challenged his thoughts</u>, and <u>used positive self-talk</u>, "Hey, I am good enough. If I say, "Hi, nice to meet you," we could have fun and possibly be friends." "I think they will like me. If not, it is ok. I will give it a try! I am Awesome!"

"I am Awesome!"

Children talking, having fun with each other and with Freddie!

Example of positive self-talk, **"Yes, we are all the same." "I am good enough." "I just have to be me and that's easy!"**

Note: No worries. It will work out! No problems. (Trying = progress). <u>Recognize your successes</u>.

Exercise: Look for self-defeating thoughts and behavior. Are they true, probably not? Check the facts.

I am a Great Friend! They would be Lucky to have Me as a Friend! _____

Communication as a Coping Skill!

Be the person you want to attract! Mirror self-love and self-confidence, followed by actions of those postive thoughts.

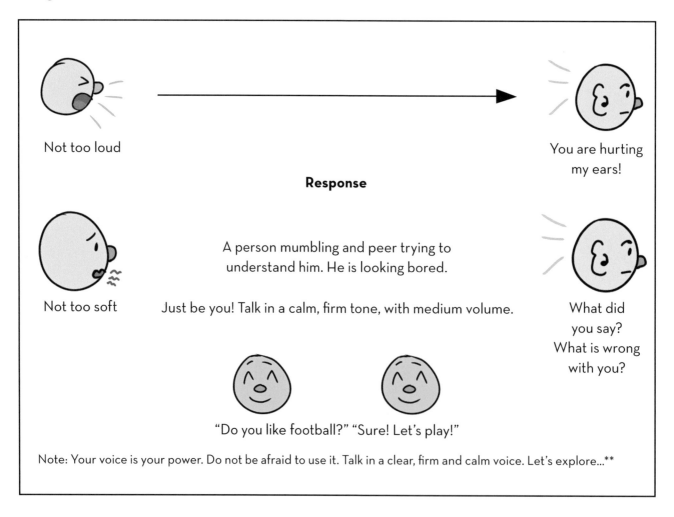

Not too loud

You are hurting my ears!

Response

A person mumbling and peer trying to understand him. He is looking bored.

Not too soft

Just be you! Talk in a calm, firm tone, with medium volume.

What did you say? What is wrong with you?

"Do you like football?" "Sure! Let's play!"

Note: Your voice is your power. Do not be afraid to use it. Talk in a clear, firm and calm voice. Let's explore...**

You are Terrific! _____

Making a Friend and Increasing Interpersonal Skills are important!

It is not always easy to connect with other people, especially during a pandemic, but it is possible. Finding common interests with others is essential. Just like matching same-to-same, which usually comes easy for most(e. g., puzzle pieces, colors, sizes and shapes, etc.). Do the same with potential friends. On the other hand, it is ok to accept the differences we see in others. That is how we learn different things, have different experiences and perspectives, in order to grow.

Note: Withholding judgment, prejudice and giving yourself time to know others' qualities are great coping skills to connect with others and develop meaningful and potential friendships.

- Here are two coping skills: <u>Self-acceptance and acceptance of others that are different from you!</u>

- Do you want more friends? Circle your answer: Yes or No.

- What qualities do you want in a friend? List here. _____

Sometimes, we attract how we feel about ourselves. This increases the chances of developing unhealthy relationships, if we ourselves are not happy and have unresolved issues. Heal yourself first, before entering new relationships. Just remember, while making friends and developing relationships, do not lose your sense of self. Be true to yourself.

- How would you make friends?_____.

Note: Assist individual/child with identifying cues, triggers and coping skills.

Exercise: Self-reflect on your past, present and desired relationships.

The Mirror Chart

Instruction: Below select past relationships. Circle your past/ previous relationships (all that apply).		Instruction: Below select present relationships. Circle your current/ present relationships (all that apply).		Instruction: Below select future/ desired relationships. Circle your desired relationships (all that apply).	
Myself	Friend	Myself	Friend	Myself	Friend

Exercise 1: Explore: Identify the pair of mirrors that reflect or matches your relationships in the past, present and relationships you would like in the future. You are column one and Friend column two.

Exercise 2: See the mirrors chart. Which reflections did you circle and why? Write answer here.

1. Past Relationship: _____.
2. Present Relationship: _____.
3. Future/ Desired: Relationship: _____.

Exercise 3: Self-Reflection

From the exercise and information provided, determine if your selection of friends have changed for you over the past. Circle your answer: Yes or No.

My Note Page:

_____

_____

_____

_____

_____

_____

_____

_____

_____

_____

_____

_____

_____

_____

_____

Journal your thoughts.

Note: Be what you expect in others.

You are Victorious!

Making a Friend and Increasing Interpersonal Skills are important!

Coping Skills:

- Connect and identify with others' likes and dislikes.
- Set and respect each other's wishes (healthy boundaries)
- Share interests and hobbies.
- Do not lose who you are, when making friends.

Note: Your friend will add to your life and you will add to theirs.

Be that person, you want in your life! (e.g., positive, supportive, a good listener, fun, brave and smart.)

- **Self-Reflect: If you want...**
  - respect- give it
  - to be a friend- be friendly
  - nicety - be nice
  - kindness- be kind
  - generosity – be giving.
  - forgiveness- forgive, etc...

Note: Be what you expect in others.

- What does it take to be your friend?
1.
2.
3.
4.

Note: Setting healthy boundaries with others will increase your chance of making friends with people who will respect you and vice versa!

- **Exercise: Practice: Role Play here!**

If you want a friend that is funny. Practice telling a joke!

Have Fun!!

You can practice writing a joke here.

You are Strong! _____

Setting Healthy Boundaries as a Coping Skill!

See the diagram/ illustration below to visualize setting healthy boundaries with a peer over the phone or social media.Consequently, you do not want to receive calls or contact from a person that you just met or someone you have known for a long time, because they are bullying you.

Explore the questions: What will you do to set boundaries? Should you block his/ her calls? Yes or No

Diagram #1.

Examine this demonstration (from right to left) of being empowered by setting healthy boundaries.

Illustration of Block the call.

	Blocked Number		(Closed Line)
Your Phone Line I say, "No more/ Stop."		Call Stopped/ No Access	Peer/ Bully's Call ⟵

Blocked Bully's Call.

Coping skills/ Consequences
1. Set healthy boundaries.
2. Keep block on.
3. Be Happy.
4. Give yourself time to know them first.
5. Do not give out your personal information to strangers.

_____

Note: Do not be afraid of rejection. You get to choose the people you want in your life.

Narration: Continue to explore the next diagram to view concrete images of setting boundaries, as a coping skill, via on social media or cellphone.

You are Strong!
Who is the Greatest? You are! _____

Setting Healthy Boundaries as a Coping Skill!

Diagram #2.

Explore the questions: Is this illustration demonstrating power, a lack of power or control of the situation? Write your answer: _____ .

Examine this demonstration (from right to left) of giving away your powered by not setting healthy boundaries.

(Open Line) Your Phone Line	UnBlocked Number Peer/ Bully's Call	Call is not stopped/Access Allowed
Unblocked Bully's Call.	←	←

Coping skills/ Consequences
1. No Block
2. No healthy boundaries.
3. Feelings of anger, frustration and anxiety
4. Fear
5. Report to someone.
6. Do not answer.
7. Yelling/ Cursing

If you do not like the inappropriate calls. What can you do? _____ .
   • Exercise:
Do you have a choice of who you communicate with or choose to be your friend? Yes or No?
Is so why?

Note: Focus on the people who are in your inner circle for support!

You are Terrific! _____

Using a Safe Phrase as a Coping Skill!

For self-awareness, it is important to <u>identify body cues and triggers to uncomfortable emotions.</u>

All emotions can be considered as useful and functional (Reframe thoughts about good and bad emotions). Some emotions make us "feel bad," that's why we sometimes ignore or block them. But the negative emotions are important too. They serve a purpose. They tell us there is a need that requires our attention.

You can <u>develop and communicate a safe phrase,</u> so that others will know you are at your limit and may need their assistance.

See the illustrations. Here is a car put putting down the street...

Note: When I am tired, I say, "I am out of gas." This is when I do not have enough energy to complete certain tasks or requests being made from myself and others. When things seem, they are getting outof control, stop and use self-care! You may regain control by implementing the necessary coping skills that work for me. These coping skills and safe phrases may vary for different people and different circumstances.

Please see the table of emotions and examples of healthy coping skills:

Identified Emotions	Coping skills to stop, reduce and manage the stressor/ trigger.
tired	ex. take a nap
anxious	ex. see doctor, be prepared, medication, therapy
nervous/shy	ex. challenge negative thoughts, friends
depressed	ex. Communicate, exercise, take medication
confused	ex. ask, research

My Note Page:

_____

_____

_____

_____

_____

_____

_____

_____

_____

_____

_____

_____

_____

Journal your thoughts.

Note: It is ok, if you get tired or cannot fulfill all of your duties. You can ask for help, use a safe phrase or use some of the coping skills listed above. Prioritize your "To do List." If you run out of time, finish your list after a nap or some self-care.

Narration: Use the work space provided to explore your "Safe phrase." Use artwork to facilitate the process, identify emotions, stressor and triggers, to regulate your mood.

You are My Hero! _____

Using a Safe Phrase as a Coping Skill!

Exercise:

*Draw your own image/ or car and develop a self-phrase, to use when tired, anxious, depressed and so on, to meet your needs.

My Car. You can also name your car.

My Safe Phrase: "_____."

Exercise: Complete the table of emotions by listing examples of your healthy coping skills below:

Identified Emotions	Coping skills to stop, reduce and manage the stressor/ trigger.
tired	
anxious	
nervous/shy	
depressed	
confused	

Note: Negative emotions tell us we have a need, that should be addressed or met. Take action and meet your own needs. Manage, reduce and/ or eliminate the efforts of stressors. The sooner you use the coping skills, the better you will feel. Care for yourself first to care for others. Let other's know you need their support.

Yes! Way to Go!

My Note Page:

_____

_____

_____

_____

_____

_____

_____

_____

_____

_____

_____

_____

_____

_____

_____

_____

_____

_____

_____

Journal your thoughts.

You are Talented! _____

Self-Awareness!

Recognize and reframe your thoughts. Uncomfortable feelings are normal, but it is best to <u>minimize them!</u> Learn to manage and process negative emotions and experiences. By identifying them, embracing them and working through them, you give yourself permission to heal, forgive and move forward. It is ok. You are ok. <u>Normalize the situation.</u>

To heal is not automatic. It will take some work and action. Healing takes time. Heal at your own time. There is no quick fix. Give yourself permission to release the pain of the past and live happily today.

Examples of facing uncomfortable feelings.

- <u>I'm scared,</u> but if I try, I can overcome my fears.
- <u>I'm tired.</u> I should sleep/ or take a break.
- <u>I'm shy,</u> but it is not a big deal. I can do it. I am good enough.

Example of using coping skills to manage or reduce uncomfortable emotions:

"I had a fight with a friend. I'm depressed. I will talk to my friend, mom or dad. I will feel better."

Coping skills: <u>Normalization</u>

It is normal to feel certain emotions (e.g., sad, depressed, anxious or disappointed), when going through particular situations. Others would feel the same way as you feel, when going through the same situation or experience. Tell yourself, "If they can pull through and make it, I can too."

List an experience when you did not think you would make it and you did!

Resilience!

Narration: Use the following diagram to facilitate self-awareness by identifying and exploring body cues and triggers of your emotion (anxiety). Then explore and develop coping skills to manage feelings of anxiety.

You are Gifted! _____

Self-Awareness!

Here is an example of using this diagram to identify body cues, triggers and coping skills for Self- Awareness: Anxiety

Identify and address body cues and triggers to shorten the length of time experiencing anxiety, uncomfortable feelings or stress.

Body cues: They are signals from your body telling you that something is wrong, something is happening or something is about to happen. My Examples: Self-awareness of anxiety

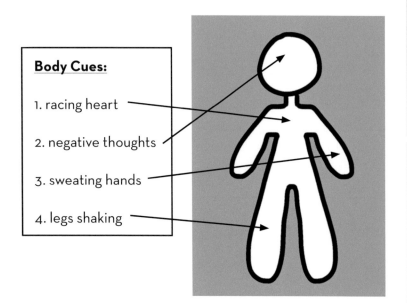

Body Cues:

1. racing heart

2. negative thoughts

3. sweating hands

4. legs shaking

Triggers: start/set off emotions

Example
1. Loud noise
2. Yelling
3.

List Coping skills to manage feelings of anxiety.

1. listen to music
2. Deep breathing
3. Exercise
4. Communicate
5.

Exercise: On the illustration above, the gingerbread man/ body diagram shows an outline with the arrows pointing to the heart, head, hand and leg according to the corresponding number. This provides a visual, to connect your mind with identified body cues, which in turn tells you to put your coping skill(s) in place. **Complete this task for each emotion, along with identifying and writing your triggers and healthy coping skills in the designated space.**

This exercise is used to increase self-awareness of your body cues and triggers, during certain situations that we often ignore.

My Note Page:

_____

_____

_____

_____

_____

_____

_____

_____

_____

_____

_____

_____

_____

Journal your thoughts.

Note: You can add other cues, triggers, and coping skills as your self-awareness increases. Just refer back to this same diagram and modify as changes occur. Sometimes, cues and triggers may change.

Narration: Use the following diagram/worksheet to facilitate self-awareness by identifying and exploring body cues and triggers of your emotion (anger). Then explore and develop coping skills to manage feelings of anger.

You are Fantastic! _____

Self-Awareness!

Self- Awareness: Anger

Identify and address body cues and triggers to shorten the length of time experiencing anger.

Body cues: They are signals from your body telling you that something is wrong, something is happening or something is about to happen.

Complete the diagram: Identify your cues and triggers to **Anger.**

Body Cues:

1. Clinched fist.

2.

3.

Triggers: start/set off emotions

Example
1. Someone yelled at me.
2.
3.

List Coping skills to manage feelings of anger.

1.Do not personalize.

2.

3.

Draw arrows from each identified body cue to each body part.

This exercise is used to increase self-awareness of body cues and triggers of anger.

Note: Assist individual/child with identifying body cues, triggers and coping skills to anger. Remember, you can add other cues, triggers, and coping skills as your self-awareness increases. Just refer back to this same diagram and modify. Sometimes, cues and triggers may change.

My Note Page:

_____

_____

_____

_____

_____

_____

_____

_____

_____

_____

_____

_____

_____

_____

_____

_____

_____

_____

Journal your thoughts.

Narration: Use the following diagram/worksheet to facilitate self-awareness by identifying and exploring body cues and triggers of your emotion (depression). Then explore and develop coping skills to manage feelings of depression.

Have a Great Day! _____

Self-Awareness!

Self- Awareness: Depression

Identify and address body cues and triggers to shorten the length of time experiencing depression.

Body cues: They are signals from your body telling you that something is wrong, something is happening or something is about to happen.

Complete the diagram: Identify your Cues and Triggers to Depression.

Body Cues:

1. Tearful

2. Withdrawn

3.

4.

Triggers: start/set off emotions

Example
1. Loss of friend.
2.
3.

List coping skills to manage feelings of depression.

1. talk to someone
2.
3.

Draw arrows from each identified body cue to each body part.

This exercise is used to increase self-awareness of body cues and triggers.

Note: Assist individual/child with identifying cues, triggers and coping skills. Remember, you can add other cues, triggers, and coping skills as your self-awareness increases. Just refer back to this same diagram and modify. Sometimes cues and triggers may change.

My Note Page:

_____
_____
_____
_____
_____
_____
_____
_____
_____
_____
_____
_____
_____
_____
_____
_____
_____

Journal your thoughts.

Narration: Use the following diagram/worksheet to facilitate self-awareness by identifying and exploring body cues and triggers of your emotion (anxiety). Then explore and develop coping skills to manage feelings of anxiety.

You are Fabulous! _____

Self-Awareness!

Self- Awareness: Anxiety

Identify and address body cues and triggers to shorten the length of time experiencing anxiety.

Body cues: They are signals from your body telling you that something is wrong, something is happening or something is about to happen.

Complete the diagram: Identify your Cues and Triggers to Anxiety.

Body Cues:

1.
2.
3.

Triggers: start/set off emotions

Example
1.
2.
3.

List coping skills to manage feelings of anxiety.

1.

2.

3.

Draw arrows from each identified body cue to each body part.

This exercise is used to increase self-awareness of body cues and triggers.

Note: Assist individual with identifying cues, triggers and coping skills. Remember, you can add other cues, triggers, and coping skills as your self-awareness increases. Just refer back to this same diagram. Sometimes cues and triggers may change.

My Note Page:

_____

_____

_____

_____

_____

_____

_____

_____

_____

_____

_____

_____

_____

_____

_____

_____

_____

Journal your thoughts.

Narration: Use the following diagram/worksheet to facilitate self-awareness by identifying and exploring body cues and triggers of your emotion (stress/ frustration). Then explore and develop coping skills to manage feelings of stress/ frustration.

I think you are Great! _____

Self-Awareness!

Self- Awareness: Stress and Frustration

Identify and address body cues and triggers to shorten the length of time experiencing stress/ frustration.

Body cues: They are signals from your body telling you that something is wrong, something is happening or something is about to happen.

Complete the diagram to identify your Cues and Triggers to **Stress and Frustration.**

Body Cues:

1. Tight muscles
2.
3.

Triggers: start/set off emotions

Example

1. Increase work
2.
3.

List coping skills to manage feelings of stress/ frustration.

1. Ask for help.
2.
3.

Draw arrows from each identified body cue to each body part.

This exercise is used to increase self-awareness of body cues and triggers.

Note: Assist individual with identifying cues, triggers and coping skills. Remember, you can add other cues, triggers, and coping skills as your self-awareness increases. Just refer back to this same diagram and modify. Sometimes, body cues and triggers may change as you change.

My Note Page:

_____

_____

_____

_____

_____

_____

_____

_____

_____

_____

_____

_____

_____

_____

_____

_____

_____

Journal your thoughts.

Narration: Use the following diagram/worksheet to facilitate self-awareness by identifying and exploring body cues and triggers of your (suicidal/homicidal ideations). Then explore and develop coping skills to manage suicidal/homicidal ideations.

Be your best You, today! _____

Self-Awareness!

Self- Awareness: Suicidal/ Homicidal Ideation

Identify and address body cues and triggers to shorten the length of time experiencing suicidal/homicidal ideations.

Body cues: They are signals from your body telling you that something is wrong, something is happening or something is about to happen.

Complete the diagram to identify your Cues and Triggers to Suicidal/ Homicidal Ideation.

Body Cues:

1. withdrawn

2.

3.

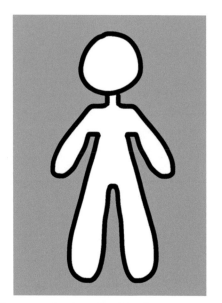

Triggers: start/set off emotions
Example

1. Loss of friend/ Break up with friend
2.
3.

List coping skills to manage suicidal/ homicidal ideations.

1. Call 911
2.
3.

Draw arrows from each identified body cue to each body part.

This exercise is used to increase self-awareness of body cues and triggers.

Note: Assist individual with identifying cues, triggers and coping skills. Remember, you can add other cues, triggers, and coping skills as your self-awareness increases. Just refer back to this same diagram and modify. Sometimes, body cues and triggers may change, as you change.

Note: If you or someone you know is at risk of suicide, please seek a professional. Call 911 or your nearest ER for help right away.

My Note Page:

_____

_____

_____

_____

_____

_____

_____

_____

_____

_____

_____

_____

_____

_____

_____

_____

Journal your thoughts.

You are Exuberant! _____

How to Deal with Suicidal and Homicidal Ideations!

Note: Suicidal Ideation/ Homicidal Ideation (SI/HI) is real. If you are at risk of harming yourself or others, or if you know someone else is at risk, <u>Get help immediately. Call 911 or go to the nearest emergency room/ (ER). Seek professional help, look and listen for signs of SI/HI, never leave the person alone, find out their location and remove potential harmful objects.</u>

There is not a magic pill for depression, mood disorders, suicidal ideation and/ or other mental health conditions/ disorders. <u>Therapy and medication</u> have been proven to be effective, if done simultaneously.

Note: Here are a few thoughts that you can rely on and practice. Challenge self-deprecating thoughts, counteract painful affect with humor, show the ironic aspect of the situation, recognize some lightheartedness, as an antidote to their sadness and recognize any successes.

Just know: You:
- **Are awesome & worthy.**
- **Deserve love.**
- **Deserve happiness.**
- **Are not responsible for what other people did to you. This is not who you are, but who they are.**

Say positive affirmations to yourself:
- **I'm ok.**
- **I am beautiful.**
- **I am the light.**

Do the following:
- **be the light in dark times.**
- **encourage yourself.**
- **love yourself.**

- use self-care.
- demonstrate self-love.
- Say, "I Love You!"
- Forgive yourself and others.

Note: For mental health issues, find a good healthcare professional (therapist and/ or doctor) that fits your needs.

My Note Page:

_____

_____

_____

_____

_____

_____

_____

_____

_____

_____

_____

_____

_____

_____

Journal your thoughts.

You are the Best! _____

Visualization as a Coping Skill!

Look past this moment and imagine your happy place!

My happy place is _____**!**

Below: Draw an image of your happy place. To visualize your "happy place," you may use a hand-drawn picture, a postcard or a photo saved on your cellphone. You can take a picture and carry the picture where ever you go or use it as a screensaver!

Note: Looking at pictures of happy times, vacations, accomplishments, and family/ friends (e.g., past and present) can be an effective tool for improving your mood. Additionally, this coping skill can assist with recognizing your successes, your joys, identifying the good times, recognizing what others have done for you and shared with you in the past. Sometimes, we forget the goodof ourselves and others, especially if we are focusing on the negatives. Let's do the opposite.

Focus on the positive!

Have a Splendid Day! _____

Would you like to be free from Negative thoughts? It is a choice only you can make for yourself!

Question: Would you like to Trash Your Negative Thoughts/ Behavior? Yes or No

Exercise: If you have a situation, behavior, person, place or thing that triggers negative emotions, write it on a piece of paper. Discuss, explore and process the event and emotion associated with it and throw it in the trashcan "for good".

Remember, it should be a conscious effort, when you release this negative thought, statement, event orperson. After disposing it (e.g., in written form or drawing), you will leave it there and do not remove it from thetrashcan. Be mindful, if you start to rehash the thought, stop and leave it in the trashcan. Remind yourself, "I threw that away." "It is gone." Instructions: Explore the negative thoughts below. Circle the thoughts youwant to throw away. Write in your own negative thoughts that are not listed.

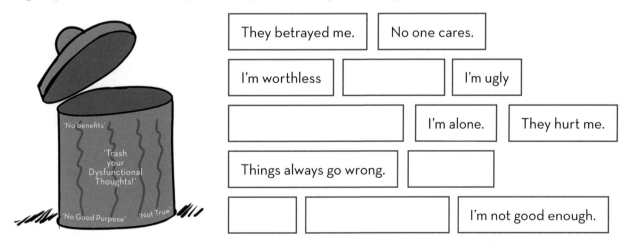

Note: Complete this demonstration with the individual, that is holding on to a negative event. (This person may be you.) Do not ask them to throw away the statement or event (what is written on the paper), until they are ready to let go, completely! Their Choice! Their Power! If the individual is unwilling to throw the negative event(s) in the trash, assist the individual with identifying and exploring their motive(s) for holding on to this negative thought, behavior, event and/ or person.

You can do it, if you put your mind to it! _____

Would you like to be free from Negative thoughts? It is a choice only you can make for yourself!

Managing your anger is important and necessary. We should not take angry feelings out on others or our loved ones.

Examples: "My mother is always telling me to do something." "My father always criticizes me." "He was never there for me." Exercise: Answer the following questions.

1. **Circle your choice. Should you challenge the negative/ absolute thoughts, throw them away or both?**
2. **Do you have negative thoughts and feelings? Circle your choice. yes or no.**
3. **Are the negative thoughts worth your time and energy? Circle your choice. yes or no.**
4. **Do you take your negative thoughts and emotions (e.g., anger, disappointment, sadness, etc.) out on others? Circle your choice. yes or no. If yes, identify who the person is, by writing their name or initials on this line _____ .**

Identify/ Explore your negative thoughts that make you feel anger with the identified person above. Then, go against these thoughts here:

Column A: Identify negative thought/ behavior	Column B: Challenge the thought to manage anger
1. She always tell me to take out the trash.	1. I take out the trash on Mondays and Thursdays.
2.	2.
3.	3.
4.	4.

Be brave enough to work through your problem issues, so you may get the life and love you deserve. If you are a parent, sometimes, you may feel guilty, even if you are doing your best. Do not do a misjustice to your child, by feeling guilty about your situation. Hold them accountable for their own actions and responsibilities. Provide support as needed, demonstrate love and allow them to work through their issues, preferably, with the support of a helping professional. Teach self-love to your child by example.

Note: Parents should protect children, without limiting a child's autonomy and growth. If you say mean words to others, you hurt yourself and them.

You did it before. You can do it again! _____

Would you like to be free from Negative thoughts? It is a choice only you can make for yourself!

Exercise: Here is a chance to be brave and self-examine.

What is your purpose, need, or motivation for exhibiting this mean/angry behavior or any behavior, toward others?

1. Attention
2. to get something (tangible item)
3. to avoid something (negative)
4. to escape something (negative or adversive)
5. or it is self-stimulating (it makes you feel good. example: rocking, shaking leg and even causing chaos and/or drama)

Exercise. Identify/ Explore your negative thoughts that make you feel anger with the identified person above. Then, explore for the motive/ purpose for the thought/ behavior here:

Column A: Identify negative thought/ behavior.	Column B: Identify purpose, need, or motivation for the behavior/thoughts.
1. ex. arguing with parent.	1. to get attention.
2.	2.
3.	3.
4.	4.

Note: To parents/ family. You brought your children here, but you are a separate individual from your children. Allow them to develop into their own authentic self. If and when they make a mistake, it is not a reflection of you or your parenting skills. As a parent, you are obligated to provide, protect from harm and offer guidance/ support. The best thing you can do to help your children, is to hold them accountable for their actions, follow up on requests, be present, show them love, demonstrate self-love, allow them to grow and have autonomy.

__Narration: Continue to use this illustration/ exercise to facilitate self-awareness of taking anger or negative emotions out on others and identify the motive or purpose for your behavior.__

You are Intelligent! _____

Meeting your needs in a Healthy Way!

Let's find healthy ways to meet your needs.

Motivations/purpose:	Some Healthy Ways:	Your New Behavior:
Attention	school: raise hand, ask to talk	
Desire something/item	communicate for what you want	
avoid something	ask for help, postpone	
escape something	express thoughts & emotions	
feel good/self-stimulation	deep breathing, challenge negative thoughts, exercise, tell a joke, acts of kindness	

Note: Manage Your Anger by identifying and dealing with your first emotion.

__Exercise: Circle the emotions that may trigger your feelings of anger.__

nervous

sad

embarrassed

tired

sleepy

threatened

hungry

shame

lonely

shy

jealous

anxious

grief

helpless

hurt

disrespected

pain

disappointed

frustrated

insecure

scared

__Narration: Use this illustration/ exercise to explore and develop healthy coping skills to manage anger.__

You are Capable! _____

Meeting your needs in a Healthy Way!

Note: Resolve those feelings and you can better manage your feelings of anger.

Explore coping skills to manage anger. Examples: Communicate, draw, exercise, face fears, etc.

Exercise: List your coping skills to managing your feelings of anger:

1.

2.

3.

4.

5.

You did It!
You completed Book II

Narration: As we come to the end of Book Two, let us continue to focus on self-awareness and healthy coping skills. Complete a summary on what you have learned overall from completing Book Two. Remember to review skills, if necessary, maintain handouts/ worksheets as a reference for future use, and practice of learned skills.

You are capable!_____

Coping skills:

Summary:

Note: <u>Challenge thoughts that make you feel depressed</u>, sad, have low self-confidence, low self-esteem and/ or feel lonely or alone.

Self-Love is key. You deserve to be happy. <u>Be mindful</u> to make decisions that make you happy, not unhappy (e.g., do homework, study, follow rules, work, be independent, listen, be on time, etc.).

You have finished Book 2. Overall, what did you learn about yourself?

1.
2.
3.

What are some healthy coping skills that will work for you and others around you?

1.
2.
3.

How is your self-awareness!

Write a Note to self on what you have learned about yourself, while completing Book II._____
_____
_____

Narration: Parent, individual and helping professionals may present this Certificate of Achievement for completion of Book Two, if skills were learned and can be implemented, as noted in the summary. Hopefully, some of the skills learned has helped the child or individual to improve their self-awareness, quality of life, and developed coping skills to assist with regulating thoughts, behavior and mood. Remember there is no quick fix, when seeking change. It is a process. Hang in there for the process. You are worth it!

Certificate

Hero Award!!
Certificate of Achievement
Awarded to:

_____

For the Completion of
Connie's Gifts -Interactive Books
and Collectibles 2 of 3

Great job on Increasing Self-Awareness and Being Brave Enough to be You! You are a true Hero!

Sign:_____ Date:_____

Title:_____

Subject Index/ Terms/ Definitions/ References

N. **Building your Self-Confidence, by Challenging and Reframing negative thoughts of self as a coping skill** (p. 59-60) Corey, Gerald, (2008) (-p. 293)

O. **Communicating/ Connecting with others.** (p. 61) Boutot, E.A, Myles, B.S. (2011).(p.205)

P. **Making friends and Increasing Interpersonal Skills / Self-Reflecting (p. 62-63)** Boutot, E.A, Myles, B.S. (2011).(p.216-219)

Q. **Setting Healthy Boundaries as a Coping Skills/ Dealing with Bullies on Social Media** (p.64-65) Raymond, R. (2015). (p.1-5); https://www.harleytherapy.co.uk/counselling/healthy-boundaries.htm

R. **Developing and Using a "Safe Phrase" as a Coping Skill (p.66-67)** V. Rodriguez, C.N., Jackson, M.L. (2020). **13,** 872–882

S. Note page (p. 68)

T. **Self-Awareness and Facing Uncomfortable Feelings (p. 69)** Boutot, E.A, Myles, B.S. (2011) (p.205)

U. **Increase Self-awareness, by identifying cues, triggers and coping skills to Anxiety, anger, depression, stress/ frustration, Suicidal/ Homicidal Ideation**. (worksheet)(p.70- 75); Cully, J.A., & Teten, A.L. 2008 (p.46)self-awareness- Corey, Gerald, (2008) 139-141); Boutot, E.A, Myles, B.S. (2011).(p.257)

V. **How to cope with Suicidal Ideation and Mental Health Issues in session (p.76)** Corey, Gerald, (2008) (-p. 294-295)

W. **Visualization, imagery and recognizing your Happy Place as a coping skill (p.77)** Corey, Gerald, (2008) (p. 253); Gladding, S.T. (2012) (p.206)

X. **Trash your negative thoughts, as an alternative/ coping skill. (p.78)** Corey, Gerald, (2008) (-p. 288-290)

Y. **Challenging negative thoughts – Worksheet (p. 79)** Corey, Gerald, (2008) (-p. 288)

Z. **Facilitate Self-awareness by identifying negative thoughts and identifying purpose/ motivation** (p. 80-81) Boutot, E.A, Myles, B.S. (2011). (p. 205)

AA. **Meeting needs in a healthy way. (p.82)** Corey, Gerald, (2008) (-p. 297-300)

Terms/ Definitions

Absolute thoughts. The tendency to think in concrete, black and white terms. (Oxford Dictionary)

Automatic thoughts. Personalized notions that are triggered by particular stimuli that lead to emotional responses. (Corey, G., 2009, p. 288)

Backwards Chaining/ Learning. Behavior linked together beginning with learning the last behavior in the sequence. (J. Cooper,2007, p436, 443)

Behavior. Acts, habits, and reactions that are observable and measurable. (Corey, G., 2009, p. 253

Challenging/Disrupting irrational beliefs. The most common cognitive method of REBT consists of the therapist actively disputing individual's irrational beliefs and teaching them how to do this challenging on their own. (Corey, G., 2009, p. 282)

Cognition. The act or process of knowing, perception. (Corey, G., 2009, p. 253). Insight, philosophies, ideas, opinions, self-talk, and judgements, that constitute one's fundamental values, attitudes and belief

Cognitive Behavior Therapy/ CBT. Aaron T. Beck founded cognitive therapy, which gives a primary tole to thinking as it influences behavior. (Corey, G., 2009, p. 9)

Cognitive Distortions. An exaggerated or irrational thought pattern involved in the onset or perpetuation of psychopathological states, such as depression and anxiety. Thoughts that cause individuals to perceive realty inaccurately. Beck, J. S. (2011).

Cognitive Triangle. Proposed by Aaron Beck. A diagram that depicts how our thoughts, emotions and behavior are all interconnected with each other and influences one another. Cully, J.A., & Teten, A.L. (2008)

Cognitive Restructuring. Is a central technique of cognitive therapy that teaches people how to improve themselves by replacing faulty cognition with constructive beliefs. Involves helping individual learn to monitor their self-talk, identify maladaptive self-talk and substitute adaptive self-talk for their negative self-talk. (Corey, G., 2009, p. 278/ Ellis,2003)

Coping skills. To acquire more effective strategies in dealing with stressful situations. (Corey, G., 2009, p.297).

Dysfunctional. (coping skills). Not operating normally or properly. (Oxford Dictionary) Unhealthy coping mechanism that bring temporary relief, joy, feeling of numbness for pain.

Forward Chaining/Learning. Behavior linked together beginning with learning the first behavior in the sequence. (J. Cooper,2007, p. 442)

Functional. (coping skills). Having a special activity, purpose, or task relating to the way in which something works or operate. (Oxford Dictionary) Permits an individual to deal directly with the stressor faced.

Generalize. To apply a behavior or skill to other conditions of interest. (J. Cooper, 2007, p. 196)

Interconnected. To connect with one another. (Oxford Dictionary)

Internalize. To keep or take something in. It can be used in either a positive or negative way. (Merriam-Webster Dictionary)

Interpersonal Skills. Relating to relationships or communication between people. (Oxford dictionary)

Intervention. Action taken to improve a situation, especially a medical disorder (Oxford Language)

Mindfulness. The process that involves becoming increasingly observant and aware of external and internal stimuli in the present moment and adopting an open attitude toward accepting what is rather than judging the current situation. (Corey, G., 2009, p. 255)

Normalization. Refers to the use of progressively more typical environment, expectations, and procedures "to establish and/or maintain personal behavior which are as culturally normal as possible." (J. Cooper, 2007, p. 59)

Positive Affirmations. Defined as positive phrases or statements that we repeat to ourselves. Generally, they are used to manifest goals, dreams or experiences we desire. Szente, J. (2007)

Positive Reinforcement. Occurs when a response is followed immediately by the presentation of a stimulus and, as a result, similar responses occur more frequently in the future. (J. Cooper, 2007, p. 258)

Psychoeducation. Premised on the idea that education is about changing perceptions as well as acquiring knowledge. Gladding, S.T. (2012).

Psychotherapy. Is a process of engagement between two persons, both of whom are bound to change through the therapeutic venture. At best a collaborative process that involves both the therapist and individual in co-constructing solutions to concerns. The counselor facilitates healing through a process of genuine dialogue with the individual. (Corey, G, 2009 p. 6)

Rational Emotive Behavior therapy/ REBT. Albert Ellis founded (REBT). A highly didactic, cognitive, action-oriented model of therapy that stresses the role of thinking and belief systems as the root of personal problems. (Corey, G., 2009, p. 9)

Reality Therapy. Focuses on individuals' current behavior and stresses developing clear plans for new behaviors. Like reality therapy, behavior therapy puts a premium on doing and on taking steps to make concrete changes. (Corey, G, 2009 p. 10)

Reframe. Putting what is known into a new, mor useful perspective. (Corey, G., 2009, p. 421)

Replacement behavior. Determining an adaptive behavior that will take the place of another. (J. Cooper,2007, p. 60)

Role playing. Role playing has emotive, cognitive, and behavioral components, and the therapist often interrupts to show clients what they are telling themselves to create their disturbances and what they can do to change their unhealthy feelings to healthy ones. (Corey, G p. 284)

Self-Care. When a person looks after their own basic health needs, without needing anyone else to help them. (Collin dictionary)

Self-Evaluate. The process or an instance of assessing oneself and weighing up one's achievements. (Collin dictionary)

Self-defeating. A plan or action that is likely to cause problems or difficulties instead of producing useful results. (Collin dictionary)

Self-deprecating. Criticize one's self or represent themselves as foolish in a light-hearted way. (Collin dictionary)

Self-disclosure. A process of communication by which one person reveals information about themselves to another. (Merriam-Webster Dictionary)

Self- exploration. Taking a look at your own thoughts, feelings, behavior and motivations and asking why. It is looking for the roots of who we are, answers to all the questions we have about ourselves. (Psych center)

Self-Love. The instinct or tendency to seek one's own well-being or to further one's own interest. (Collin dictionary)

Solution-Focused Brief Therapy. Postmodern approach, challenges the basic assumptions of most of the traditional approaches by assuming that there is no single truth and that reality is socially constructed through human interaction. A systemic theory with focus on how people produce their own lives in the context of systems, interactions, social conditioning and discourse. Shifts the focus from problem solving to a complete focus on solutions (Corey, G, 2009 p. 11, 377)

Therapy. The treatment of disease or disorder, as be some remedial, rehabilitating or curative process. (Merriam-Webster Dictionary)

Transference. The displacement of affect from one person to another, the projection of inappropriate emotions onto the leader of group member. Gladding, S.T. (2012).

Triggers. An event, person or situation that makes something else happens.

References

A. Beek, A.T. (1976) Cognitive Therapies & Emotional Disorders. New York: New American Library

B. Beck, J. S. (2011). Cognitive behavior therapy: Basics and beyond (2nd ed.). New York, NY, US: Guilford Press.

C. Boutot, E.A, Myles, B.S. (2011). Autism Spectrum Disorders. Foundations, Characteristics, and Effective Strategies. Pearson Education, Inc., Upper Saddle River, New Jersey.

D. Burns, D.D, (2012) Feeling Good: The new mood therapy. New York: New American Library

E. (Cooper, J. O., Heron, T. E., & Heward, W. L. (2007). Applied Behavior Analysis (2nd Edition) Prentice Hall.

F. Corey, Gerald, (2008) Theory and Practice of Counseling and Psychotherapy (8th Edition). [Brooks/Cole.

G. Cozby, P. C. (2007). Methods in Behavioral Research (9th Edition) The McGraw. Hill Companies, Higher education.

H. Durlak, J.A., Furnham, T. and Lampman, C. (1991).; Stallard, P. (2002).

I. Crosson-Tower, C. (2008). Understanding Child Abuse and Neglect,7th Edition. Harvest Counseling and Consultation. Pearson

J. Gladding, S.T. (2012). GROUPS, A Counseling Specialty, (6th Edition). Pearson Education, Inc.

K. McKay M & Fleming, P. (2016) Self-Esteem: A Proven Program of Cognitive Techniques for Assessing, Improving & Maintaining Your Self-Esteem. New York: New Harbinger Publications.

L. Miltenberger, R. G., (2008). Behavior Modification. Principles and Procedures (4th Edition). Wadsworth Cengage Learning.

M. Therapy aid.com

N. Umbreit, J., Ferro J., Liaupsin, C. & Lane, K., (2007) Functional Behavioral Assessment and Function-Based Intervention, An Effective, Practical Approach. Pearson Merrill Prentice Hall.

O. Raymond, R. (2015). 12 Signs You Lack Healthy Boundaries (and Why you Need Them). Harley Therapy, April 2, 2015, Counseling, Relationship.

P. Rosenthal, H. (2008) Encyclopedia of Counseling, (3rd Edition). Master Review and Tutorial for the National Counselor Examination, State Counseling Exams and the Counselor Preparation Comprehensive Examination.

Q. Stallard, P. (2002). Think Good-Feel Good.

R. Sue, D.W., and Sue D. (2008). Counseling the Culturally Diverse. Theory and Practice (5th Edition). John Wiley & Sons, Inc.

S. Stanovich, K. E., (2007). How to Think Straight About Psychology (8th Edition). Allyn and Bacon, Pearson Education, Inc.

T. Q. Cully, J.A., & Teten, A.L. 2008. A Therapist's Guide to Brief Cognitive Behavioral Therapy. Department of Veterans Affairs South Central MIRECC, Houston.

U. Szente, J. (2007). Empowering Young Children for Success in School and in Life. *Early Childhood Educ J* **34,** 449–453 (2007). https://doi.org/10.1007/s10643-007-0162-y

V. Tilindiene, I., Rastauskiene, G.J., Gaizauskiene, A. & Stupuris, T. (2012). Relationship Between 12-16-year-old athletes' self-esteem, self-confidence and Bullying. Ugdymas. Kuno. Kultura. Sportas. Nr. 2 (85); Socialiniai Mokslai, Lithuanian Academy of Physical Education, Kaunas, Lithuania (p. 76-82).

W. Kisner, J. (2017). The Politics of Conspicuous Displays of Self-care. The New Yorker. (p.1-5). https://www.newyorker.com/culture/culture-desk/thepolitics-of-self-care.

X. Greimel E, Kato Y, Müller-Gartner M, Salchinger B, Roth R & Freidl W (2016) Internal and External Resources as Determinants of Health and Quality of Life. PLoS ONE 11(5): e0153232. https://doi.org/10.1371/journal.pone.0153232. https://doi.org/10.1371/journal.pone.0153232

Y. Rodriguez, C.N., Jackson, M.L. (2020). A Safe-Word Intervention for Abduction Prevention in Children With Autism Spectrum Disorders. *Behav Analysis Practice* **13,** 872–882 https://doi.org/10.1007/s40617-020-00418-x

Printed in the United States
by Baker & Taylor Publisher Services